DK SUPERGUIDES
SWIMMING

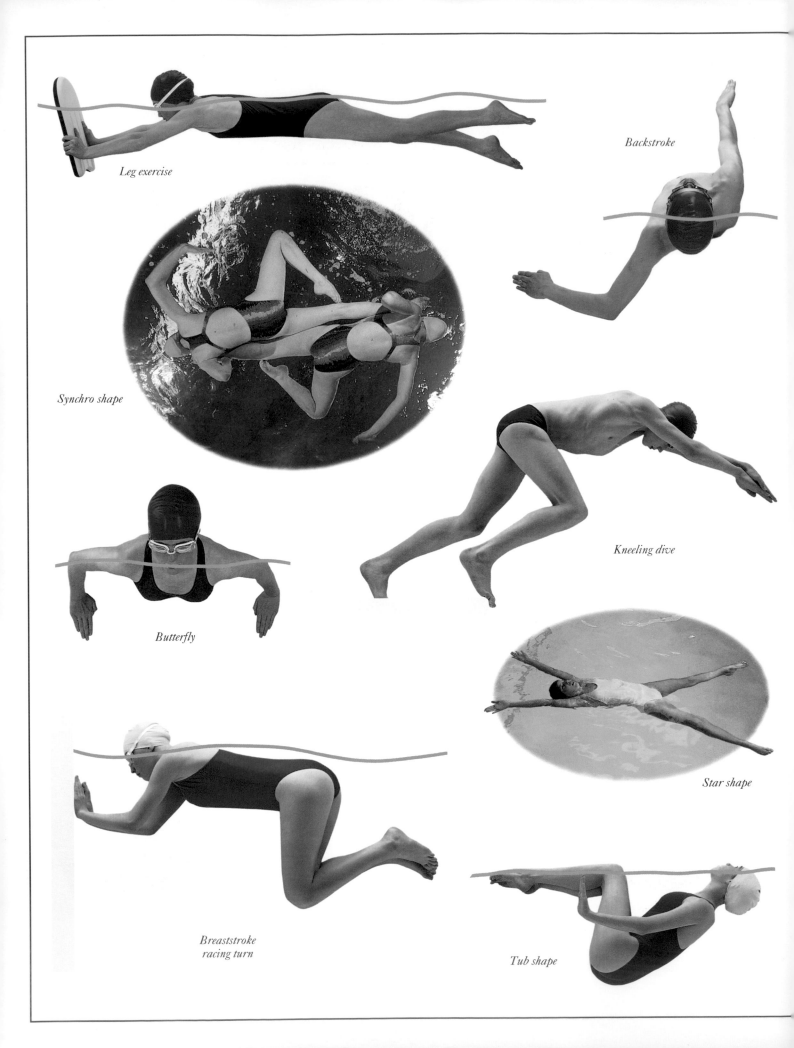

Leg exercise

Backstroke

Synchro shape

Kneeling dive

Butterfly

Star shape

Breaststroke racing turn

Tub shape

Adjusting goggles

Ready to swim

DK SUPERGUIDES

SWIMMING

Written by Rick Cross
Foreword by Jeff Rouse

Forward somersault

Alternating arms

Crawl

DK PUBLISHING, INC.

www.dk.com

A DORLING KINDERSLEY BOOK

DK www.dk.com

Project editor Lee Simmons   **Project art editor** Penny Lamprell
Editor Elinor Greenwood   **Art editor** Rebecca Johns
Photography James Jackson
DTP Designer Almudena Díaz
Picture researchers Mollie Gillard and Andrea Sadler
Production Josie Alabaster and Orla Creegan

The young swimmers

Harry Bond, Annabelle Halls, Marvin Jones, Jun King, Greta McLachlan,
Lisa Morrison, Laura Mulford, Kaya Ramjee, Melanie Stables

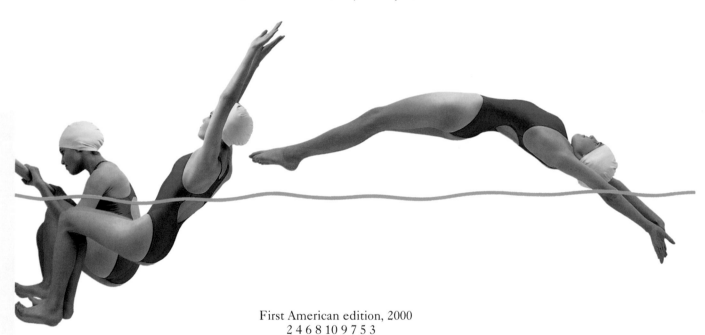

First American edition, 2000
2 4 6 8 10 9 7 5 3

Published in the United States by
Dorling Kindersley Publishing, Inc.
95 Madison Avenue
New York, NY 10016

Copyright © 1997, 2000
Dorling Kindersley Limited

First published as *The Young Swimmer*, 1997

ISBN: 0-7894-5432-7

Color reproduction by Colourscan, Singapore
Printed and bound in Italy by L.E.G.O.

Contents

10
To all young swimmers

11
History of swimming

12
Starting swimming

14
Where to swim

16
Basic know-how

18
Early skills

20
On the move

22
The crawl

24
Backstroke

26
Breaststroke

28
Butterfly

30
Racing starts

32
Racing turns

34
Synchronized swimming

36
Events and
competitions

38
Taking it further

40
Water safety

42
Glossary

44
Index and acknowledgments

To all young swimmers

NO MATTER who you are or where you live, swimming is a rewarding activity to learn. This sport can provide you, as it did me, with the skills necessary to propel you through life; goal setting, time management, work ethic, and self-confidence are several of these important qualities. Swimming is a full-body exercise that provides you with excellent physical conditioning. But swimming is fun, too, as anyone can tell you who has spent the afternoon floating, splashing, and playing in the pool. Confidence in the water can also lead to other endeavors such as water polo, waterskiing, and surfing. I hope that after reading this book you will appreciate how exciting and enriching swimming can be as a hobby, or a career.

Jeff Rouse

"The home stretch of any race never looks easy!"

"Participation in the Olympics was always a dream of mine, so with a gold around my neck all I can say is 'thumbs up' to a dream come true!"

"Believe it or not, I have a great time during workout!"

"The start of a race is my first opportunity to shine, so I make sure my form and focus are sharp!"

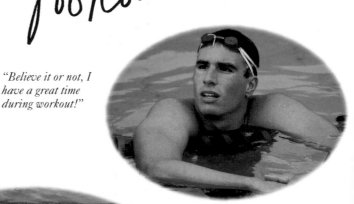

"After this great swim in Phoenix, Arizona, in 1996, I knew I was one step closer to winning an Olympic gold medal."

History of swimming

ANCIENT CARVINGS found in the Middle East suggest that people have been able to swim for over 4,000 years. Swimming began as a survival skill, and only really became popular as a sport in the 19th century. Early strokes included the breaststroke, sidestroke, and various forms of the crawl. The butterfly was the most recent stroke to be invented. It was used in breaststroke races until 1952, when it became an event in its own right.

Swimming with pig bladders
This stone frieze from ancient Iraq, dating from 869 B.C., shows warriors crossing a river using inflated animal bladders and breathing tubes. The arm action is quite similar to that used in front paddle.

A popular pastime
Swimming was very popular in the early 19th century. Changing rooms lined the edges of the pool and swimming was segregated into men or women only.

Weissmuller went on to become a film actor, starring as Tarzan.

Johnny Weissmuller
Weissmuller was one of the most famous American swimmers. In the 1928 Olympics he won nearly all the sprint titles. Because of improved methods of communication, his swimming actions were recorded, studied, and copied around the world.

Mark Spitz
At the 1972 Olympic Games in Munich, Germany, US swimmer Mark Spitz established himself as one of the greatest swimmers of all time. During the games he won seven individual events, all in world record time. He also swam in three team relay events.

Spitz at the 1972 Olympics. During his career he set 26 world records.

A typical man's bathing suit from 1921.

Printed stripes improve the flow of water over the body.

The close-fitting Acquablade legsuit is for men and women.

Suit design
Swimsuits have come a long way since the beginning of the century. Then, swimsuits were made of wool and were cumbersome and heavy. Today, advances in technology have resulted in fabrics that help to make swimmers more streamlined and drastically improve their speed.

Starting to swim

T O START OUT in swimming all you really need is a swimsuit and a towel. However, if you plan to swim regularly with a team you will also need some of the items shown here. A sweatsuit, or other warm clothing, pool shoes, a cap, and goggles are important. Later, your coach might suggest using equipment such as kickboards and pull buoys. Ask your coach about the kind of food you should eat. You should certainly consider using a plastic drinking bottle if you start training sessions.

A cap makes you more streamlined in the water.

Swimmers wear swimsuits two sizes too small to streamline their bodies.

An extra towel may come in handy during training sessions or when attending swimming events.

Swimsuit
To cut down on drag in the water it is important that your swimsuit is the correct size and fits snugly. Most teams have their own team outfit in the team's colors, which members can buy.

Joining a team
Join a team to get expert advice on how to improve your swimming skills, and also to get the opportunity to take part in competitions. Inquire at your local pool or write to your nearest swimming association (see page 45) for information. Visit a team and watch the coaches at work to see what a training session involves.

Sweatsuit
Wear your sweatsuit to keep warm before and after training and also between swimming events at competitions. Your sweatsuit should be loose and comfortable.

Caps make it easy to identify team members in the water.

A swimsuit with a close-fitting high neck cuts down on drag.

Keep a plastic drink bottle handy in your bag.

Always change into pool shoes when at the pool since outdoor shoes are unhygienic.

You can store clothing and other equipment in a bag.

Basic equipment
Your coach will help you decide what equipment you need.

Handholds

Pull buoys
These two types of pull buoys are specially designed for arms-only work. They fit lengthwise between your legs, just above your knees.

Kickboards
Kickboards are useful buoyancy aids for legs-only work. They will help you improve your technique if you are starting out. If you already swim, they can help you strengthen your legs.

Paddles and mitts
Use hand paddles or hand mitts for extra arm strengthening work. Make sure they are the correct size for your hands.

Hand mitts

Hand paddles

The flexible material enables you to change your hand shape.

Weighted dive rings
Dive for rings to practice swimming underwater with your eyes open.

Chamois towel
A chamois towel is very absorbent, drying you quickly and efficiently.

Nose clips stop water from going up your nose.

Goggles
Goggles will protect your eyes from pool chemicals and will help you see more clearly in the water.

Tuck loose ends of elastic into headstrap.

1 To put goggles on safely, hold the eyepieces on your eyes with one hand and hold the strap with the other.

2 Stretch the strap over the back of your head and position it comfortably just above your ears.

Where to swim

SWIMMING IS THE perfect way to have fun and stay in shape. All you need to do is find out where your local pool is. You can take swimming lessons here, or join a local club. Pools have changing rooms, lockers for clothes and valuables, showers, footbaths, and lifeguards. Many pools have sides higher than the water level. Others are called "deck level" because the water washes over the edges. Competition pools are usually 50 m (164 ft) long with separate diving areas.

Open-water swimming

Open-water swimming and other water sports are very enjoyable, especially if you follow basic water safety rules (see pages 40-41). Make sure you are a strong swimmer, and don't go swimming alone. Learn the meaning of warning flags and buoys. Ask lifeguards for information about water conditions.

Outdoor pools

While many international venues are indoors, some countries with a warm climate have open-air pools. The 1991 European Championship, were held at this outdoor pool in Athens, Greece. Here, a training session for the event is in progress.

Lane markers

Lane markers are used to stop people from swimming into each other's paths. Some are called antiwave markers because they have discs which stop waves, or backwash, from spreading into another swimmer's lane.

A third color change is a warning that the pool end is only 5 m (16 ft) away.

Discs alternate between two colors along the length of the pool.

The plastic discs are threaded over a wire.

Competition pools

This picture shows Ponds Forge in Sheffield, England. As with some competition-size pools, it has movable booms at each end, so the length can be adjusted from 25 to 50 metres (82 to 164 ft). The pool also has an adjustable floor so that it can be used for a large variety of swimming competitions, water polo, or synchronized swimming.

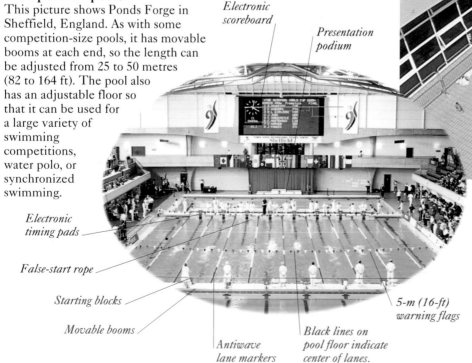

Electronic scoreboard

Presentation podium

Electronic timing pads

False-start rope

Starting blocks

Movable booms

Antiwave lane markers

Black lines on pool floor indicate center of lanes.

5-m (16-ft) warning flags

Diving rules

1.8 m

Diving into the water head-first can be very dangerous, so it's important to follow certain rules.

• DO take notice of pool depth markers.

• DO go through the proper learning stages with your coach before diving.

• DO NOT attempt a racing dive in water less than 1.8 m (6 ft) deep.

Warning signs
Warning signs, such as flags and boards, can be seen posted by lifeguard patrol stations and along the beach. They mark out the areas where you can or cannot swim (see page 40).

Warming up/Cooling down
• Always allow sufficient time for both.

• Warming up before you swim should be both exercises on land and a water workout.

• Cooling down afterward brings your heart rate back to normal and helps you recover.

Nutrition
A car can't run without the right fuel and neither can you!

• Eat well on the day of a competition to give your body energy.

• Eat soon after a competition to replace lost energy.

• Drinking fluid, such as water, is essential. Drink a little at a time, but often.

Backstroke flags
Flags strung across the pool 5 m (16 ft) from each end warn backstroke swimmers that the pool end is near.

50-meter pool

Spectator stands

Diving areas have a minimum depth of 3.5 or 5 m (11 or 16 ft), depending on the board heights.

Diving boards of different heights

Competition officials stand by the lanes and check the timing, finishing order, and whether finishes are legal.

Leisure pools
Some pools are leisure or fun pools. These have features such as wavemaking machines and long, spiraling slides or chutes. The chutes are made slippery by constant running water.

Starting block
For safety reasons blocks are fixed to the poolside and the top is made of nonslip fiberglass. The top slopes down to the front to help swimmers launch off smoothly. Speakers are inserted into the blocks so that all the swimmers hear the starting signal at the same time.

Rails used for backstroke starts.

Basic know-how

Cheat at the beginning by gently paddling with your hands.

IF YOU ARE JUST starting out in swimming, trying these floating and gliding exercises will increase your confidence in the water. Start with the mushroom float, then try out different shapes, such as the star float or horizontal float. Floating and making different shapes on your front or back will show you how the shape you make in the water affects your balance.

Horizontal float
Try to get your body as level as possible with the surface, with your head just resting in the water.

Star float
Stretch out on the surface as if you were lying on a clock face with your arms at about 10 o'clock and 2 o'clock and your feet at about 4 o'clock and 8 o'clock. If you find the float difficult, try it on your front first. Keep your head level with your body.

Mushroom float
This float is sometimes called a jellyfish float. It is a good exercise to start with if you are trying to float for the first time. Take a deep breath, lower your face into the water, then tuck your legs in tightly and hug them close. After sinking a little, you will gradually rise to the surface.

Floating
Breathe in and out very gently so that your lungs stay full of air and keep you afloat.

Push and glide on your front

Push and glide is a useful skill to learn as it encourages you to stretch out and find the most efficient body position for gliding.

Keep your head down.

Push and glide
These skills will help when you begin to learn starts and turns.

3 Now push off vigorously, stretching both legs out behind you. Glide along the surface with your arms and legs outstretched and your face in the water.

2 Bounce gently off your standing leg and place both feet side by side on the pool wall.

1 Stand with your back to the wall. Place one foot firmly against it and bend your other leg slightly. Stretch out your arms and hold on to the front of the kickboard, with your thumbs on top.

Hands on top
Another way to hold the kickboard is to put your hands over the leading edge and rest your arms lightly on the upper surface of the kickboard.

From lying to standing

From your front

When you first glide on your front without a kickboard, you might find it difficult to stand up afterward. Try to think of the following points as you are about to leave your glide position.

Plant your feet firmly on the bottom.

Exercising Try this first when you are close to the pool wall.

1 Raise your head and press downward and backward with your hands at the same time. Your legs will then start to sink.

2 As your legs start to sink, bend your knees and bring them up toward your chest.

3 As your body rotates, your feet will begin to point downward. Lower your legs and stand up.

From your back

Traveling backward is less natural than traveling forward, so you will find that standing up after gliding on your back is an important skill to learn.

1 Drop your chin onto your chest and circle your hands backward until they are level with your shoulders and close to the surface.

2 As your legs sink, bend your knees into your chest and scoop your hands toward your feet.

3 As you rotate, swing your knees under you, and point your feet downward. Lower your feet and stand up.

Push and glide on your back

Practicing push and glide on your back will help you improve your backstroke start or turn.

Holding one kickboard

Try this exercise with just one kickboard, too. Hold the sides of the kickboard and lay it flat along your thighs at arms length.

Standing up If you want to stand up, it is easier if you let go of the kickboard and scoop your arms and hands as shown above.

Keep your hips up when gliding.

Keep your chin tucked in.

1 Stand facing the wall, holding a kickboard under each arm. Bounce gently as you lean back to plant both feet firmly against the wall, just under the surface.

2 Push off strongly and straighten out both legs, stretching your body out. Try to keep the back of your head just resting in the water, with your ears at surface level.

Early skills

HAVING GAINED confidence in the water, you can try some more advanced activities. One of the most important swimming skills you can learn is sculling. All swimming strokes make use of sculling actions in some way. Just by changing the angle of your wrist you can travel head first, feet first, or even stay in one place. Sculling is also needed to perform other skills, such as treading water or somersaulting.

Stationary sculling

Sculling is a continuous action. Lie on your back and stretch out your hands, keeping your fingers together. Angle your palms out and down and, leading with your little finger, trace a figure eight with your hands.

Your little finger always leads.

Your thumb starts and ends by your thigh.

Somersaults

Somersaults in the water help you practice getting your bearings when upside-down, as well as being fun! Knowing how to do somersaults will also help you when you start to do racing turns.

Forward somersault

When performing a forward somersault, it is easier to begin from a horizontal position on your front.

1 From your front, kick vigorously down with both legs together in a dolphin kick. At the same time, drop your chin onto your chest.

2 Begin to bend your knees and bring them forward toward your chest.

3 As your knees come forward, bend your arms and, turning your hands palms-up, push upward. This will start you rotating into your somersault.

Tuck your knees in tightly.

4 While you are upside-down and still rotating, turn your palms to push toward your feet. This will help you to continue turning.

5 Remain in a curled-up position as you are turning. Your palms should continue to push toward your feet.

6 Continue pushing with your hands. As your head comes around to the surface, open out onto your front again.

Figure eight

Trace a figure eight, moving your hand away from, then toward, your body. As your hand nears your thigh, your thumb should be facing up, although your little finger still leads. Now rotate your hand so that it travels around the bottom curve of the eight to start again.

Figure-eight movement

Treading water

You will need to know how to tread water if you stop to rest in deep water, or if you need to gather your bearings in open water. Hold your arms out in front of you and scull with your hands, sweeping outward and inward.

Keep your hands close to the surface.

Your legs work in a gentle, vertical breaststroke kick.

You can also try moving your legs as if you are riding a bicycle.

1 From lying in the water on your back, drop your head backward into the water, bend your knees, and begin to press your hands downward and backward.

Backward somersault

To prevent water from going up your nose as you somersault backward, slowly bubble air through your nose while you somersault. Alternatively, you can wear a nose clip.

6 Look for the surface, then begin to open out onto your back again.

Bring your knees to the surface.

2 To continue to rotate backward, push down with your hands. Your feet will pass over your head.

Look for daylight above you.

Keep pushing your head backward.

3 As you rotate, you will pass through a sitting position under the water. Press down with your palms and lift your hips toward the surface.

5 Scoop your hands down and back and continue to lift your knees.

4 Continue pressing down with your palms and lift your knees toward the surface.

On the move

TRY OUT SOME of the water confidence exercises shown here before you learn the main swimming strokes. Activities such as opening your eyes underwater, blowing bubbles, and breathing in and out as you lift your head in and out of the water will help you to become more familiar with the feel of the water.

Rolling
This simple rolling exercise will make you aware of a new way to move in the water. Take up a gliding position, with back stretched. Now, by using only the muscles in your back and abdomen, roll over onto your side, then onto your front, and finally return to your back.

Log roll
This exercise is sometimes called a log roll. Try to do one quickly without stopping. Can you turn in the opposite direction too?

Surface dive
One way of submerging efficiently is to use a headfirst surface dive. The advantage of this dive is that the first arm action can be part of a swimming stroke, usually breaststroke. You should not wear goggles when doing this dive.

1 From a swimming position, pull down with your hands and begin to bend at your hips. Breathe in just before you lower your head and pull down.

Keep your legs straight along the surface.

Begin to pike, or bend, at the waist.

Underwater games
To familiarize yourself with both breathing and seeing underwater, try these games with friends in the shallow part of the pool, away from any diving.

Swimming through legs
Take turns swimming through your friends' legs. Try to avoid coming into contact with their legs.

Making faces
Practice opening your eyes underwater by seeing who can make the silliest face.

Practicing your surface dive
Diving for rings on the bottom of the pool is a good way to practice your surface dive. You could even form teams with other swimmers and have a relay competition.

Do not challenge others on how long you can stay underwater.

Traveling through the water

How you move through the water depends on how you use your arms and hands, and legs and feet. An important rule to remember is that for every action, there is an equal and opposite reaction. If you push back, you will move forward; if you push down, you will lift up.

Start from a glide.

Kick your legs up and down alternately.

Front paddle

Knowing how to swim front, or "doggie," paddle will help you when you get to the crawl. It is an easy stroke since your hands stay under the water and you can swim with your head above the water, but it is more efficient to keep your head lowered.

Pull one arm back at a time, pushing the water for propulsion.

While one arm recovers, the other arm propels you along.

Use your hands as paddles.

2 Bend at the hips and sweep your arms toward your legs until they are parallel. Then turn your hands so that your palms press down toward the pool bottom.

Lift your legs.

3 As you press down with your hands, raise your legs, keeping them together and straight.

Back paddle

Back paddle is one way of traveling on your back. Push off on your back from a wall, and make small movements from your wrists and elbows with both hands.

Push the palm of your hand toward your feet.

Thumbs face up

Kick your legs up and down alternately.

Turn your palms down.

Press your palms downward and stretch toward the pool bottom.

4 When your legs are pointing straight up, your hands should be pointing to the floor of the pool. The weight of your legs above the surface will start to drive you downward.

Breathing exercise

If you can't breathe comfortably when swimming, your speed and the distances you can cover will be limited. The two main breathing methods are explosive and trickle; you either blow the air out quickly or let it trickle out slowly. Practice each method while standing in shallow water to decide which is best for you.

Start breathing out before your mouth clears the water.

Concentrate more on blowing air out hard than on breathing in.

21

The crawl

THE CRAWL IS the fastest and most efficient of all the swimming strokes. To swim it correctly, your body must be streamlined and horizontal, and your legs and arms must move continuously. Each arm, in turn, propels you through the water. At the same time, your legs kick up and down to keep you balanced. Your face stays in the water, even when you turn to breathe. In competition, there is no actual event called the crawl, but it is the most common choice of stroke in the freestyle event.

Arm position

1 Turn your left hand so your thumb enters the water first, palm angled out and down. Your arm should be bent slightly and close to your body's center line. Turn rather than lift your head to breathe.

Turn your face back into the water.

2 Once your hand is in the water, push it backward like a paddle, bending your elbow. Rolling slightly to your left will help you keep your hand close to the center line.

When to breathe in
Michelle Smith, the Irish Olympic gold medalist, turns her head toward the arm leaving the water. She opens her mouth wide and takes a deep breath in behind the bow wave before turning her head back to face downward.

How to breathe out
You can either use "trickle" breathing, gradually letting the air out while your face is still in the water, as shown here, or "explosive" breathing, when you blow the air out very hard just as you turn your head out of the water to breathe in.

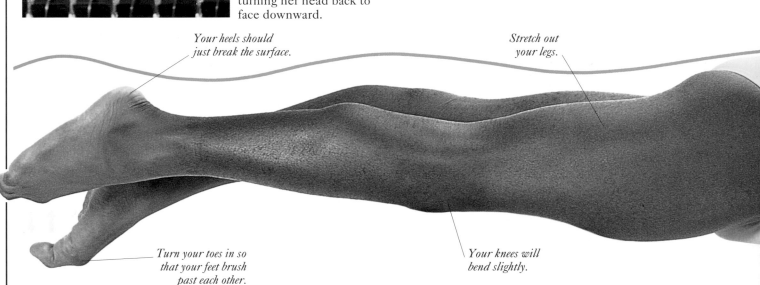

Your heels should just break the surface.

Stretch out your legs.

Turn your toes in so that your feet brush past each other.

Your knees will bend slightly.

Coordination

Kick your legs up and down alternately at all times.

Keep your feet close to the water's surface.

1 As you stretch your left arm out in front of you, turn your head to the right, take a quick breath in, then turn your face back into the water. As your right hand exits, by your thigh, your body should roll to your left.

2 As your left hand sweeps down and back through the water, turn your palm to face your feet. As your right hand travels over the water your upper arm should pass close to your ear.

3 As your left hand moves back toward your thigh, reach your right hand forwards, ready for entry.

Alternate arms
Your right arm alternates with your left arm in exactly the same way.

Keep looking forward and down.

3 As your left hand moves down and back toward your thigh, begin to straighten your elbow.

4 As your left arm straightens, brush your thumb past your thigh. Lift your left elbow so that it leaves the water first, before your hand. Turn your hand so that your little finger leads.

Leg strengthening
For this exercise, kick hard, up and down, starting the movement from your hips and finishing it with a whiplike action at your stretched ankles and feet.

Warming up
To increase the flexibility of your shoulders and spine, try this exercise. Place one hand over the back of the other, stretch your arms above your head, then gently bend from side to side, keeping your body straight.

5 As you raise your left elbow and hand clear of the water, roll your shoulders toward the hand entering the water.

Exercising
Always ask for your coach's advice before doing any exercises.

Keep your elbow high as your arm leaves the water.

Keep your face in the water at all times.

Streamlined body
Imagine a straight line running down the center of your body, from your forehead to your feet. Try to keep your hands and feet as close as possible to this imaginary line at all times. Rolling your body toward the hand leaving the water will help. Turn your head just enough to allow you to breathe.

Your body will roll naturally toward the arm entering the water.

Breathe toward the arm leaving the water.

Keep your fingers close together.

Bend your elbow as you lift your arm.

Keep your shoulders level with your head.

4 As your left hand passes your thigh, it should be turned so that your little finger leads. Lift your left elbow so it leaves the water first, followed by your hand. Your right hand enters the water and starts to pull your body along.

5 As your left arm travels forward, try to keep both hands close to the center line. To do this, bend your elbows and roll your shoulders toward the hand entering the water.

Backstroke

BACKSTROKE is not as fast as the crawl or butterfly, but it is still the fastest method of traveling on your back. You should aim for a streamlined body position, while inclining your body slightly to keep your kick under the water. Make sure that your arms and legs move continuously at all times.

Keep your head still throughout.

Focus on a line or mark on the ceiling to help you swim in a straight line.

Body roll
Practice rolling your body and shoulders toward your entering arm. This will place your entering hand into a better position for propulsion and your exiting hand into a better position for recovery.

Alternate arms
Your arms should work continuously, your right arm alternating with your left.

Streamlined
Here you can see Jeff Rouse swimming in the backstroke event at Phoenix, AZ, 1996.

"My hips and body are rotating toward my arm that is about to enter the water. This rotation helps me keep my body in the most streamlined position possible."

Straighten your knees on the down kick.

Stretch your feet and ankles.

Bend your knees slightly on the upkick.

Your legs kick diagonally as your body rolls.

Intoeing
Your feet will make more efficient paddles if you turn them inward, so that your big toes brush past each other.

Breathing
Practice breathing in as one arm recovers and out as the other arm recovers.

Coordination

Right arm is in recovery.

Arm remains straight until catch point.

Hand at catch point.

1 This sequence explains the efficient bent arm, or "S" pull. Keep your left arm in line with your shoulder as your left hand enters the water. Your little finger leads, palm facing out and arm fully stretched. Your right arm should be about to exit.

2 Once your left hand is in the water, turn your palm to face down and stretch your hand forward, down, and out to catch point, 6-8 in (15-20 cm) below the surface. Roll your body toward your left arm as your right arm begins its recovery over the water.

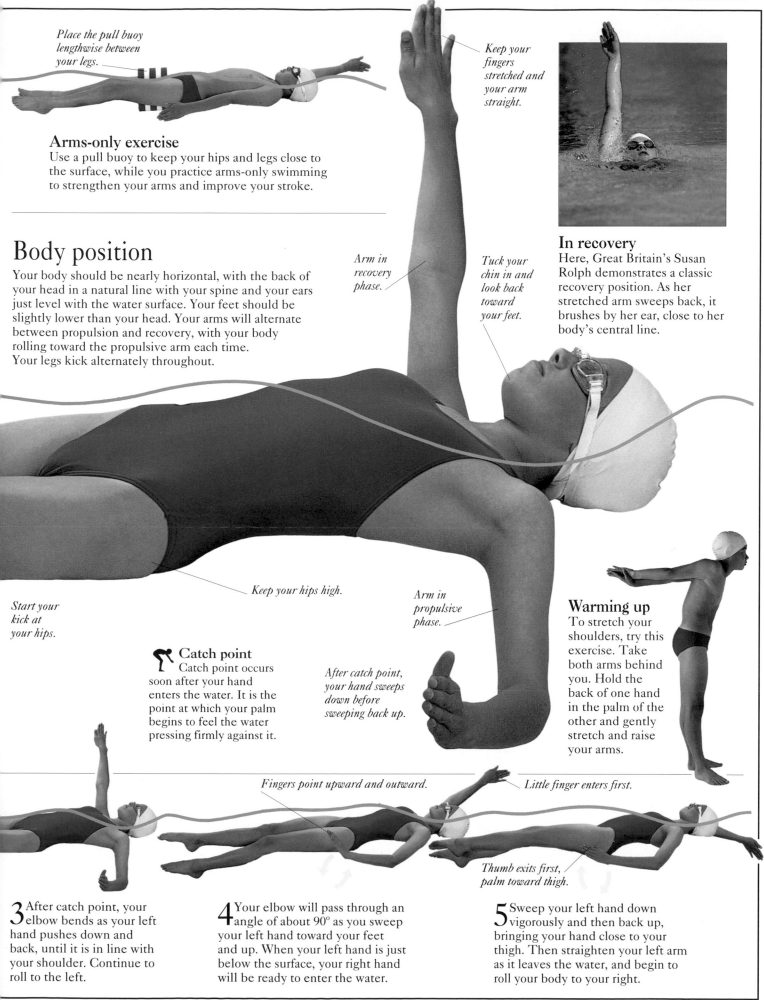

Arms-only exercise
Use a pull buoy to keep your hips and legs close to
the surface, while you practice arms-only swimming
to strengthen your arms and improve your stroke.

*Place the pull buoy
lengthwise between
your legs.*

*Keep your
fingers
stretched and
your arm
straight.*

Body position
Your body should be nearly horizontal, with the back of
your head in a natural line with your spine and your ears
just level with the water surface. Your feet should be
slightly lower than your head. Your arms will alternate
between propulsion and recovery, with your body
rolling toward the propulsive arm each time.
Your legs kick alternately throughout.

*Arm in
recovery
phase.*

*Tuck your
chin in and
look back
toward
your feet.*

In recovery
Here, Great Britain's Susan
Rolph demonstrates a classic
recovery position. As her
stretched arm sweeps back, it
brushes by her ear, close to her
body's central line.

*Start your
kick at
your hips.*

Keep your hips high.

*Arm in
propulsive
phase.*

Warming up
To stretch your
shoulders, try this
exercise. Take
both arms behind
you. Hold the
back of one hand
in the palm of the
other and gently
stretch and raise
your arms.

Catch point
Catch point occurs
soon after your hand
enters the water. It is the
point at which your palm
begins to feel the water
pressing firmly against it.

*After catch point,
your hand sweeps
down before
sweeping back up.*

Fingers point upward and outward.

Little finger enters first.

*Thumb exits first,
palm toward thigh.*

3 After catch point, your
elbow bends as your left
hand pushes down and
back, until it is in line with
your shoulder. Continue to
roll to the left.

4 Your elbow will pass through an
angle of about 90° as you sweep
your left hand toward your feet
and up. When your left hand is just
below the surface, your right hand
will be ready to enter the water.

5 Sweep your left hand down
vigorously and then back up,
bringing your hand close to your
thigh. Then straighten your left arm
as it leaves the water, and begin to
roll your body to your right.

Breaststroke

IN BREASTSTROKE, your arms and legs stay under the surface all the time. This means you have more water resistance to overcome and it is the main reason why breaststroke is the slowest of the four strokes. It is an easy, enjoyable stroke to learn since you can raise your head above the surface to breathe. Practice the leg kick while holding a kickboard, before adding the arm actions.

Exercising
Try to spread your knees just wider than hip width as you drive your legs around and back. This way, your legs will recover faster and will be ready to give you more propulsion sooner.

Keep your feet below the water surface.

Your legs propel you through the water.

Keep your knees well behind your hips.

Coordination

Keep your body streamlined.

1 Start from a good, fully stretched push-and-glide position with your ears squeezed between your arms. Try and get into this position between each full stroke. Your coach might advise you to reduce this glide as your swimming improves.

Hands at catch point.

Point your toes backward.

2 From the glide, sweep your hands outward to a point just wider than shoulder width, then turn your palms down. This point is known as catch point. The rest of your body remains in the same position as before.

Breaststroke competition
Here, swimmers can be seen using the "high-lift" style in the women's breaststroke event at the International Swimming Cup in 1990. Nowadays, many swimmers use this style to improve their speed.

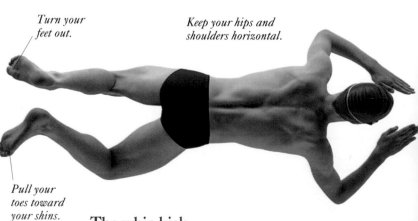

Turn your feet out.

Keep your hips and shoulders horizontal.

Pull your toes toward your shins.

The whip kick
The whip kick helps you get the most out of the powerful thrust of your legs. After bringing your heels up close to your buttocks, with your knees about hip-width apart, turn your feet up and out and kick vigorously around and back.

Body position
To swim breaststroke well, angle your body from your shoulders, so your feet stay under the surface. As you push your legs back and around, your arms should be stretching forward, with your head almost under the surface.

Keep your head in a streamlined position.

Breathe in as your hands come beneath your chin.

Stretch your arms forward as far as you can after breathing.

Incline your body downward slightly.

Keep your hips just below the surface.

The high-lift style
Here, Krisztina Egerszegy of Hungary swims breaststroke by lifting her upper body out of the water and moving her hips up and down in a wave-like action. This reduces water resistance, helping her swim faster.

Bring your heels toward your buttocks.

Breathe in as your head and shoulders rise.

Drop your hips.

Drive your legs around and back.

3 After catch point, bend your elbows sharply so that your palms sweep around, down, and back. Gradually start lifting your head and shoulders forward and up and begin to bend your knees.

4 Continue to bend your elbows and circle your hands. After they pass below your elbows, begin to bring them up toward your chin. Turn your feet up and out, ready to drive back.

5 Stretch your arms forward, and return to the original glide position, lowering your head back so you are streamlined once again.

After catch point
Once your hands have reached catch point, they begin the propulsive stage. Press your hands out, down, and back as you begin to bend your arms.

Arm action
In order to improve your propulsion through the water keep your shoulders horizontal and your elbows high. Sweep your hands back and in toward your chest, pushing against the water as you do so.

Thigh and ankle warm-up
Supporting yourself against a wall, hold your foot and slowly and gently pull it back to your thigh.

Butterfly

BUTTERFLY WAS INVENTED in the early 1930s but was swum as a version of breaststroke until 1952, when it was officially recognized as a new stroke. Originally the kick was similar to that used in breaststroke, but now the more efficient up-and-down "dolphin kick" is used. Because your arms recover over the water and your legs and body undulate there is far less resistance and more propulsion than in breaststroke.

Arm position

Arms should be almost stretched.

After catch point, move your hands down, back, and in toward your body.

1 Your hands enter the water about shoulder-width apart, thumbs first and palms angled outward. Your face should be in the water.

2 After entry, sweep your hands outward to catch point, just outside your shoulders, then bend your elbows.

Coordination

1 As your hands enter the water, kick down, starting your kick from your hips. The downbeat will cause your hips to rise. Keep your ankles and toes stretched.

Butterfly race

Notice the powerful arm recovery of the swimmers in this picture, which shows the men's butterfly event at the International Swimming Cup, Rome, Italy 1990.

2 Continue to kick down as your hands reach catch point, just outside your shoulders. Your hips are still rising.

Stretch your ankles and toes.

Keep your ankles stretched.

Turn your toes in slightly.

3 Begin raising your legs in an upbeat as your hands sweep inward, toward your body's center line. Your face remains in the water, but your head rises a little. Start to drop your hips.

Taking a breath

Here, Hayley Lewis of Australia is about to lower her head back into the water after breathing, but before her arms finish their recovery.

4 As your hands continue sweeping in and back, your legs are still on the upbeat and your head keeps rising. Your hips continue to drop.

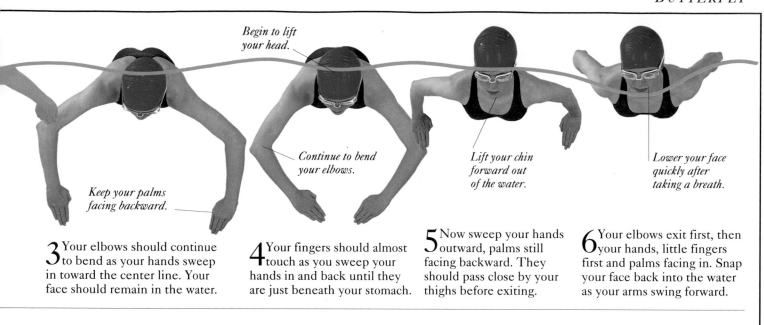

Begin to lift your head.

Keep your palms facing backward.

Continue to bend your elbows.

Lift your chin forward out of the water.

Lower your face quickly after taking a breath.

3 Your elbows should continue to bend as your hands sweep in toward the center line. Your face should remain in the water.

4 Your fingers should almost touch as you sweep your hands in and back until they are just beneath your stomach.

5 Now sweep your hands outward, palms still facing backward. They should pass close by your thighs before exiting.

6 Your elbows exit first, then your hands, little fingers first and palms facing in. Snap your face back into the water as your arms swing forward.

Body position

To swim butterfly well, your body should undulate in a wavelike fashion, alternating between a level, streamlined position and a more inclined position, with your hips high and breaking the water's surface. The head rises up above the water at the end of the underwater arm action.

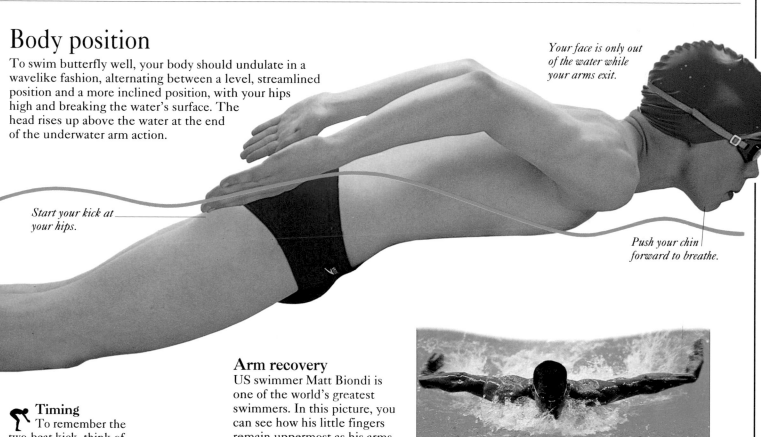

Your face is only out of the water while your arms exit.

Start your kick at your hips.

Push your chin forward to breathe.

Arm recovery
US swimmer Matt Biondi is one of the world's greatest swimmers. In this picture, you can see how his little fingers remain uppermost as his arms swing around clear of the water during the recovery.

Timing
To remember the two-beat kick, think of kicking once as your arms enter the water and again as they exit.

Your hips start to rise.

Sweep your arms out wide.

5 As your hands sweep outward past your thighs, ready to exit, your legs start to move back down through the water.

6 As your arms recover over the water, your legs finish their downbeat and start rising again and your hips begin to drop.

Warm-up
This exercise stretches your shoulder and upper arm. Gently pull your elbow across and down your back. Repeat with the other arm.

Racing starts

MAKING A strong start in competitions is vital, especially for swimming short distances. You need to get away from the starting block quickly and accurately judge your flight distance and the angle of entry into the water.

Kneeling dive
A kneeling dive is a good dive to learn first. Position yourself carefully so that you don't slip as you push off. Grip the pool edge with the toes of your front foot. You should travel both up and outward.

Curl your toes.

Place your knee by your front foot.

Hold your hands and stretch your arms forward.

Over-balance and stretch up, out, and forward.

Grab start

The grab start is the most common start for freestyle, breaststroke, and butterfly races, since it helps you get away from the block quickly.

6 ft (1.8 m)

Bend your knees slightly.

1 At the command "Take your marks," bend down and hold onto the front of the block. Keep your hips above your knees.

2 On the word "Go!" pull sharply on the block. As you over-balance, push off hard with your legs to gain height and distance.

3 At the top of your flight, pike, or bend at the waist. Make sure your head is down as you go into the pike.

Drive hard from the block.

Keep arms and legs fully stretched.

Grip the edge firmly with your toes.

Hand positions
You can either hold the edge of the block with your hands between your feet, or just outside them.

Rules
Ask your coach to explain the competition rules on racing starts.

Other starts

Windup start
Windup starts are used in relay takeovers because you judge your takeoff by the speed of the incoming swimmer. Make a big circular movement up and back with your arms, then drive off powerfully with your legs.

Track start
This start gives a bigger push off. Grip the block with your hands and toes and put your weight on your back foot. Next, pull hard with your arms and push with your feet.

Transition
The crawl
The transition is the time you are underwater between entry and the first arm stroke. Make use of a powerful dive by continuing to stretch.

1 After entry, hold your stretched and streamlined position and flatten out. Then begin to stretch upward in a glide. You will still be traveling at speed.

Keep your body stretched and streamlined.

6 ft (1.8 m)

Breaststroke
Your underwater arm pull in breaststroke is very strong, so the transition is deeper and longer than in front crawl.

1 Your entry should be slightly steeper than crawl position. After entry, flatten out into a glide.

Keep your stretched, streamlined position.

Backstroke start

Swing your arms past your head.

Stretch out your arms by your ears.

2 On the starting signal, throw your head up and back. At the same time, swing your arms up and out and push off hard with your legs.

3 Stretch out, arch your back, and reach toward the water with your fingers. Your fingers should enter the water first.

1 Hold the rail and bring your feet up high. Bend your arms and pull your chin to the rail.

Backstroke start

The backstroke start begins in the water and is really a backward dive. Face the wall and hold onto the start rail, feet close to the surface. On the word "Go!" push off, stretching up and outward. Do a few kicks underwater before surfacing to start your arm action. For safety, always look behind you before you practice this move.

4 Open out from the pike by raising your legs. Stretch forward and downward toward your entry point.

1996 Olympics

This picture shows the start of a backstroke event. Each swimmer's flight is perfectly streamlined as they reach backward toward entry.

5 As you enter the water, continue to stretch forward and downward. Your hands enter the water first followed by your body, which passes through the "hole" in the water that your hands have made. The impact of the water will be considerable, so keep fully stretched.

The fully stretched and streamlined position for entry.

🤸 **Safety**
Make sure the water is at least 6 ft (1.8 m) deep if performing headfirst dives. Check with a lifeguard, coach, or parent before diving.

Your entry should be as stretched and streamlined as possible.

The angle at which you enter the water will affect your transition into a stroke.

2 Just as you begin to slow down, use your legs to drive you up to the surface.

3 Begin your first arm action just before you break the surface. Delay breathing for a couple of strokes.

Start your leg action before your arm action.

Start your stroke as soon as possible.

2 As you begin to slow down, make a powerful double arm pull out, around and back to your hips. Follow this with a short glide.

Hold the glide position.

3 After the glide, keep your hands close to your chest as you move them forward in recovery, ready for the first stroke on the surface.

Butterfly transition

This is similar to breaststroke, except it is shorter and shallower. You use a dolphin kick followed by a powerful double arm pull to bring you to the surface.

Racing turns

GOOD TURNS CAN save you valuable time during a race. Make use of your swimming speed as you approach the wall so that you can rotate quickly before planting your feet for a powerful push off. Crawl and backstroke turns include a somersault, while breaststroke and butterfly turns require more of a twisting movement and both your hands and feet touch the wall. Crawl turns are often called "flip" turns, and the breaststroke and butterfly turns are sometimes called "touch" turns. Good turns only come through a lot of practice and hard work.

Backstroke turn

Crawl and backstroke turns are very similar. Use the 16-ft (5-m) warning flags overhead as a guide for when to start your turn.

Bring your recovering arm out of the water and across your body's center line.

Roll over.

Bring your leading hand back to your thigh.

Glide underwater, making use of the push.

Push off forcefully on your back.

Plant your feet on the wall and stretch your arms forward.

Tuck your chin in and flip your legs over.

Crawl turn

To determine the best moment for starting a turn you'll need to experiment with starting at different distances from the wall. To begin with, try starting the somersault at about 3–5 ft (1–1½ m) from the wall, then adjust it according to your results.

The push off
To get the most out of your turns, practice the push offs on their own, then you can add them to the turn.

Approach the wall at normal speed.

Keep your legs close together and parallel to the water surface.

Tuck your knees in to speed up your somersault.

1 At 3–5 ft (1–1½ m) from the wall, leave your trailing hand by your thigh and pull your leading hand back so that it is also by your thigh.

2 Turn your palms to face the pool bottom. To start the somersault, press your hands downward, drop your chin toward your chest, and do a dolphin kick with your legs.

3 Flip your feet out of and over the water. You should be faceup under the water, with your hands beginning to move forward toward your head.

Flip turns
It is vital that competition swimmers know how to do fast, efficient turns.

4 Plant your feet against the wall, under the water, then push off as hard as you can, stretching out your arms and pressing them against your ears.

5 As you push off, turn onto your front. Glide, making the most of your push-off speed, then kick your legs and aim for the surface.

Glide underwater and prepare to start the stroke.

Start to turn onto your front during the push off.

Plant your feet firmly, with your knees bent.

Push off, stretching your legs and toes.

Butterfly approach
On approach, make the touch with your arms almost at full stretch.

Hands
Overlap and lock your hands as you stretch your arms out underwater. This will make you more streamlined.

Stretch out into a glide, making the most of your push-off speed.

Breaststroke and butterfly turn

The approach, turn, and push off for the breaststroke and butterfly turn are very similar, except that during the underwater transition of the breaststroke turn you are much deeper in the water.

Stretch forward, keeping your shoulders level.

Touch the wall with both hands at the same time.

Bring your knees in as your hips move forward.

Lift the other hand out of the water and forward.

Take one hand back and turn your head.

Push off by straightening your legs while turning onto your front.

Plant your feet firmly on the wall.

Synchronized swimming

IF YOU LIKE swimming, gymnastics, and working out to music then synchronized swimming is the sport for you. If you learn the basic sculls first, you can progress on to making different shapes in the water that are called figures. In time, you will be able to combine the strokes, sculls, and figures and put them to expressive music.

Sculling practice
Locking ankles
Once you have mastered basic sculling, you can work with a partner. Link feet with your partner, squeezing your legs together. One partner performs a torpedo scull while the other performs a standard scull with their arms at their sides.

Using bottles
Buoyant plastic bottles will help keep you afloat while learning how to make different shapes with your body. Practice the flamingo position, shown here. Try to keep the extended leg straight.

Sculling

Sculling is a very important skill to learn. The movement starts from the shoulder. Sweep the palms of your hands away from your sides, little finger leading, and toward your sides, thumb uppermost. Try to keep your wrists firm, arms straight, and the movement continuous.

Point your fingers down, flexing from the wrist.

Reverse scull

Keep your hands in line with your forearm.

Flat scull

Point your fingers up. Keep your arms close to your body.

Standard scull

Canoe scull
To travel headfirst, lie on your front, with your body arched, your hips low, and your chin and feet at the surface. Stretch out your arms, keeping them close to your hips, and use a standard sculling action.

Point your fingers downward.

Torpedo scull
To travel feet first, lie on your back with your legs together, your stomach in, and your hands above your head, shoulder-width apart. Press your arms and hands down into the water and use a standard scull, fingers pointing down.

Figures

A figure is a series of movements. All figures have different names, such as "oyster" and "tub." Once you have mastered good sculling techniques, you can combine these skills to make a sequence of shapes with your body, to create figures.

Oyster

1 Start with a flat scull on your back. Keep your head, hips, and feet at the surface. Keep your hands close to your hips and your toes pointed.

2 Lift your feet and drop your hips. Keep your body straight. Press your hands down and swing them around, behind your head.

Keep your arms and legs straight.

3 Lift your legs up and circle your arms around to touch your ankles.

Hold the oyster position until you are fully underwater.

Tub

Extend your head back in the water.

Keep your knees above your hips.

1 Do a flat scull on your back. Make sure your head, hips, and feet are at the surface, and scull evenly with your hands close to your hips.

2 Drop your hips down as you bend your knees and bring your lower legs up parallel to the water's surface. Turning toward your left shoulder, complete a full circle by doing a standard scull with your right hand and a reverse scull with your left hand.

Turn the tub figure by sculling with your hands.

Formations

As a synchronized swimmer, you can perform alone, with a partner, or in a group. This gives you the opportunity to make many different kinds of formations. You can use formations both on the water's surface and underwater. It is vital that you have mastered the basic skills before performing formations with other people.

Side bent-knee link

Scull next to your partner, head to toe. Link together by holding each other's ankles close to your shoulder. Bend your outside leg, as shown here and point your toes so that your big toe touches your straight leg. Now do a standard scull with your outside arm to turn headfirst, or a reverse scull to turn feet-first.

Dolphin chain

This formation is performed underwater. Hold your partner's feet with one or two hands. Make sure you keep your body firm, your back arched, and your legs squeezed together. To turn the rotation, scull with one hand while you hold on with the other.

Open side bent-knee link

Start with a side bent-knee link. Roll onto your side to face outward and extend and straighten your inside arm. To turn the formation, do a standard scull. You can either keep your heads above or below the water.

Flat sculling will help you hold the cartwheel formation.

Squeeze your buttock muscles to keep your body arched underwater.

A nose clip will stop water from going up your nose when underwater.

Keep your body straight.

🤸 **On the surface**
A dolphin chain can be performed at the water's surface, too.

Cartwheel

When doing formations in a group, you can make numerous shapes. To make a cartwheel, form a circle. Everyone's left leg should be touching in the middle of the circle. Each person bends their right leg and places it on the hip of the person to the right.

Point your toes

Ballet leg

Practice this position with bottles before you try sculling.

1 Do a flat scull on your back. Keep your hips and feet close to the surface. Extend your head, but keep your face above the surface.

2 Draw one leg up along your opposite thigh until your bent thigh is at right angles to your body. Keep the opposite leg straight.

3 Straighten the bent leg and bring it out of the water to make the ballet leg movement. Keep your body and other leg horizontal.

Events and competitions

A S A COMPETITIVE sport, swimming has a very strong following, from swimming clubs through to district, national, and international championships, culminating in the quadrennial Olympic Games. Swimming at the Olympics is part of the aquatics program, along with synchronized swimming, water polo, and diving. The international rules are governed by the Fédération Internationale de Natation Amateur (FINA), which has over 160 member countries.

Heats and finals
Heats are swum if there are too many competitors in an event. The winners swim in the final. The fastest has the middle lane, the second and third fastest have lanes on either side, and so on, resulting in the familiar arrowhead or "V" shape.

Relay races
There are two types of relay event – the freestyle relay and the medley relay. Each "leg" of the race is completed when the swimmer in the water touches the pool end. The medley relay must be swum in the following order: backstroke, breaststroke, butterfly, and freestyle.

The outgoing swimmer must be ready to leave the block the instant the touch is made.

Triathlon
A newly created Olympic sport, the triathlon consists of three stages – swimming, cycling, and running. The Olympic distances are a 1.5-km swim, a 40-km bike ride, and a 10-km run. There are no stops between the three legs. Hundreds of competitors can enter a triathlon, and the races often start with a splash, like in this picture.

Individual medley race
A swimmer needs to excel in all four strokes to be successful in the individual medley. Competitors must swim an equal distance of each stroke in the order of butterfly, backstroke, breaststroke, and freestyle. The length of the leg is determined by the competition.

Swimmers move from stroke to stroke without getting out of the water.

Proud winners of club medals.

Swimming for gold
As a member of a swimming club, you will get the chance to take part in club championships, then perhaps interclub competitions. Eventually you might compete at national level. All international swimmers start out as, and remain, club swimmers.

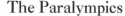

The Paralympics
The Paralympics are held every four years, and take place in the same country as the Olympics. Swimming is one of the top sports in the Paralympic Games. The swimmers are grouped together according to the level of their disability. International swimming rules are followed with only a few exceptions, such as the use of signals alerting blind swimmers of an upcoming turn or relay.

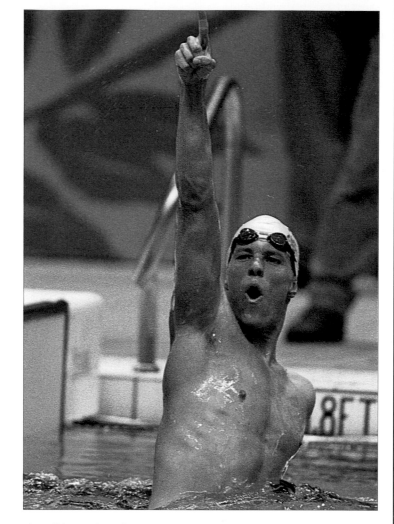

An Olympic win
The Olympic swimming program comprises men and women competing in 16 events each. There are four different strokes across a range of distances, and each race has a maximum of eight swimmers. There are preliminary heats, then the fastest swimmers go through to the semifinals, and then the finals. There is no greater thrill or reward for a swimmer than winning an Olympic gold. Here, world-record holder Kieren Perkins of Australia is elated after winning the 1500-m freestyle event at the Atlanta Olympics in 1996.

Beth Botsford shows off her gold medal in the backstroke event at the Atlanta Olympics.

The Olympic Games
Olympic swimming has come a long way from the first modern Olympic Games held in Athens in 1896. Then the event began with swimmers dropped off in the Mediterranean having to swim back to shore. Swimmers nowadays enjoy hi-tech pools, with temperature control and lane markers designed to reduce turbulence. Swimming has a status as one of the Games' glamour events and is one of the most popular spectator sports.

Taking it further

ONCE YOU CAN SWIM, a host of other new sports are opened up to you. Water sports are exciting, challenging, and varied. A water sport can be a hobby, a competitive sport, or even become a way of life. Whether you get your thrills from riding a wave, launching yourself off a high board, or playing fast-paced team games, there is something for all water-lovers. Water polo and diving can often be learned in your local pool as part of the swimming program. Windsurfing, surfing, and waterskiing have their own clubs and associations and operate on amateur and professional levels.

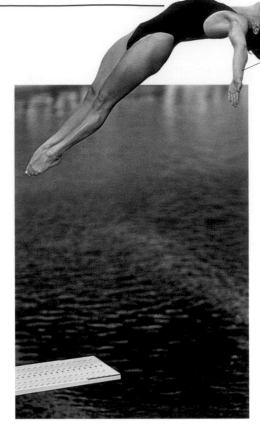

An elegant back dive.

Diving

This is a very demanding sport, requiring considerable practice and dedication. It combines the skills of a gymnast and trampolinist with the grace and poise of a dancer. It became an Olympic sport in 1904 and since then has, literally, changed by leaps and bounds. There are competitions for both men and women, and there are two disciplines: springboard, at 1 m and 3 m, and high (firm) board at 10 m. Depth of water is very important, and you should check with your local pool to find out if it is safe to learn there.

Snorkeling

With the aid of a mask, snorkel, and fins, you can float around effortlessly, breathing steadily through your snorkel pipe. The underwater world of colorful fish, turtles, and beautiful coral gardens opens up before your eyes. To follow a fish, or look at something interesting, you can dive down to the bottom for a closer inspection. If you enjoy snorkeling, you could go on to learn scuba diving.

This snorkeler is diving down to explore.

Surfing

Surfing is a spectacular and exciting sport, practiced by over 17 million people in 70 countries worldwide. All you need is a surfboard and some waves. There are international surfing competitions, though most surfers see their sport more as a way of life. Many surfers are beach-lovers, who enjoy the excitement of coming into contact with the forces of nature. Some travel all over the world on a quest for the ultimate wave. Surfing has given rise to other sports – skateboarding, snowboarding, and windsurfing. All these sports offer adventure, challenge, and excitement.

Water polo

This Olympic sport was originally played in rivers and harbors, but is now played in swimming pools with a ball similar to that used in soccer. The modern game, with seven players per team along with a number of substitutes, requires considerable swimming skill. Water polo players need to be able to swim fast for short bursts, as well as have the endurance to last for four seven-minute quarters. In addition, they need to be able to catch and throw on the move. Standing on the bottom, or holding the side of the pool, is not allowed.

Getting a grip on the dynamic world of windsurfing.

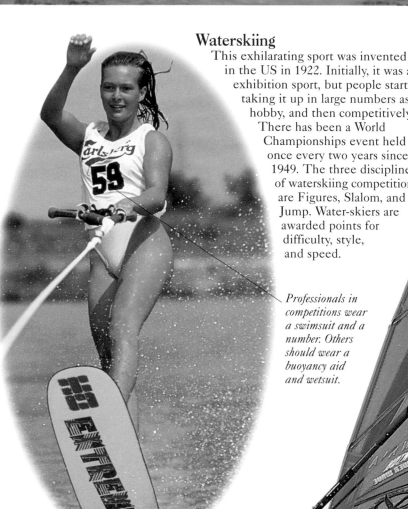

Waterskiing

This exhilarating sport was invented in the US in 1922. Initially, it was an exhibition sport, but people started taking it up in large numbers as a hobby, and then competitively. There has been a World Championships event held once every two years since 1949. The three disciplines of waterskiing competitions are Figures, Slalom, and Jump. Water-skiers are awarded points for difficulty, style, and speed.

Professionals in competitions wear a swimsuit and a number. Others should wear a buoyancy aid and wetsuit.

Windsurfing

This sport combines aspects of both surfing and sailing and can be practiced anywhere there is wind and water, by individuals of all ages and athletic abilities. The sail is attached to a mast and the windsurf board, and is maneuvered to catch the wind and speed you along. Balance and an understanding of the wind are advantageous, but anyone can learn. No matter how good you are, there is always a new skill to learn. This is one of the reasons windsurfing is so addictive!

Water safety

LEARNING TO SWIM is the single best way to make yourself safe around water. However, swimming in a heated indoor swimming pool is very different from swimming outside. Over 80% of all drownings occur outdoors, in rivers, lakes, flooded quarries, ponds, reservoirs, and the sea. It is therefore important that you know some water safety and rescue skills. A simple code, with four golden rules, will help you develop some lifeguarding sense. Remember it, and when you are out and about, your knowledge may help you become a real life-saver.

1 Take advice

Listen to the weather forecast before setting off for a swim. It may be warm and sunny inland, but when you get to the coast the weather can be different or change suddenly. One of the biggest dangers to swimmers is the cold. Make sure you don't stay in the water too long and have a towel and warm clothes handy for when you get out. Always follow the advice of lifeguards, read all signs, and learn to recognize the flags shown here.

A checkered flag means surfboards only.

A red flag means don't swim.

A red over yellow flag means there is a lifeguard on duty.

On the beach
This beach is a good place to swim. The flag means there is a lifeguard on duty, and the black and white sign shows where it is safe to swim. Enjoy the beach but take care.

2 Check for dangers

Before you make a dash for the water, make sure you've checked that the place you've chosen to swim is safe. Don't jump into very shallow water, imagining it to be deep. And don't go out of your depth if you're not a strong swimmer. The depth of water can be very deceptive.

A busy harbor
This picture shows an example of where NOT to swim. There is no lifeguard, the water may have strong currents and be very cold and deep, and there are lots of boats milling around. It is dangerous to swim near boats, or off boats. You could be in danger of being hit by one, and they create currents in their wake that can pull you under.

Littering
Sharp rocks, cans, and glass in the water can cut your feet, so wear shoes to protect them. And don't leave any litter behind...

3 Don't swim alone

Nobody should ever swim alone – not even lifeguards! Swim with your friends and family, and you'll have lots of fun. Always make sure someone knows where you are going, and when you'll be back.

4 Know how to help

It is important that you know what to do in the event of an emergency. If you see someone in trouble, stay calm and get help as quickly as you can.

Shout!
Shout loudly, not only to attract the attention of people nearby, but also try and guide the person in trouble to safety with clear instructions.

Throw a rope or something which floats – a ball, plastic bottle, or life buoy.

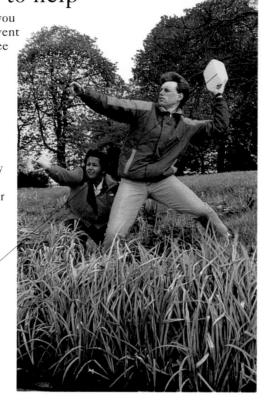

Emergencies
Try to help from the shore or land. Never put yourself at risk.

How to make an emergency float

Practice making a float from a pair of lightweight trousers. This skill will not only improve your water confidence, it could also help you cope in an emergency.

1 While treading water, soak the trousers in the water and tie a knot in the end of each leg.

Practice this exercise in your local pool.

2 Hold the trousers out by the waistband. Take a breath and pass the trousers behind your head. You may bob under the water, so keep holding your breath. Kick hard with your legs to keep afloat.

3 Keep hold of the waistband in both hands. Throw the trousers up and over your head to catch as much air as possible in the legs. Repeat until the trouser-legs are full of air.

4 Hold the waistband closed together and pull it just below the surface of the water. Rest your chin on your hands and let the float hold you up. Lie in the water and try to keep as still as possible.

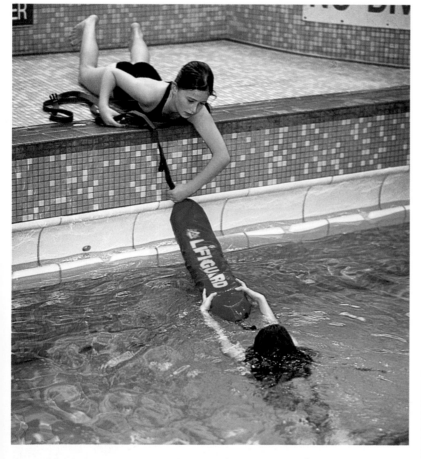

Reaching out
Reach out with a stick, scarf, sweater, or anything long, but make sure you are secure. The girl in this picture is practicing lifesaving techniques in her local pool. She has thrown out a float to pull someone in and has secured herself by lying down.

Lifejacket

A lifejacket is essential if you are taking part in some water sports. It will keep you afloat and upright, with your head out of the water, if you accidentally fall in. You should wear a lifejacket even if you are a strong swimmer.

Glossary

During swimming practice, or when watching swimming events, you may find it helpful to understand the meaning of some of the following words and terms:

Sculling

A

Action Any movement of the limbs in swimming. For every action you perform there is an equal and opposite reaction.

Alternating strokes A term used to describe the crawl strokes.

B

Backstroke start A start for backstroke races. It begins in the water and is similar to a backward dive.

Ballet leg A movement in synchronized swimming when one leg is lifted straight out of the water vertically, leaving the other leg horizontal at the water surface.

Somersault

Body roll A movement of the body toward the entering arm in the crawl and backstroke.

C

Catch point The point at which the hand starts to exert pressure on the water. This occurs soon after the hand enters the water.

Competition pool A pool used for competitions, usually 50 m (164 ft) long. Sometimes there are movable booms and pool floors, so the length and depth can be adjusted.

D

Dive ring A weighted ring that is thrown into the pool to be picked up. It is used to practice swimming underwater with your eyes open.

Diving area A diving pool, where the minimum depth is 3.5 or 5 m (11 or 16 ft), depending on the diving board heights.

Dolphin chain A formation in synchronized swimming where two back-to-back swimmers hold each other's feet, arch outward, and rotate.

Dolphin kick An up-and-down kick used in butterfly when both legs kick together.

Drag Resistance in the water. A loose swimsuit may cause drag in the water and slow you down.

E

Entry point The point where a part of your body first breaks the surface of the water.

Explosive breathing A breathing technique where air is blown out quickly and forcefully before a new breath is taken.

F

False-start rope A rope used to stop swimmers if the starter decides that a race has started without his or her consent.

Figures A series of movements to make shapes with your body in synchronized swimming.

Finals The final race of an event that decides the overall winner. The fastest swimmers from the heats (see heat) go forward to the final.

Freestyle relay A swimming race where four swimmers each swim a leg, or section, using any stroke.

Front paddle A very basic swimming stroke that uses an alternating crawl-style leg kick and a paddling arm action. Also known as "doggie paddle."

G

Glide position A streamlined body position where the arms are outstretched close to the head. A glide can be performed on the water's surface or below it, and on the front or back.

Grab start
The most common start in freestyle, breaststroke, and butterfly races. The competitor bends over and presses his or her hands against the starting block to begin the start.

H

Hand mitt A mitt made out of flexible material, that fits on to your hand and enables you to change your hand shape in the water; useful for arm-strengthening work.

Hand paddle A board that fits onto your hand and enables you to change your hand shape in the water; useful for arm-strengthening work.

Heat A race within an event. When there are more competitors than lanes in a pool, the competitors are divided into groups, or heats. Each group swims a heat and the swimmers with the fastest times go through to the finals.

High-lift style A style of breaststroke used by many swimmers to increase their speed.

Horizontal float A floating position when the swimmer's legs are together and arms by the side.

I

Intoeing A position of the feet, when they are turned inward to give greater foot extension and make the foot a more effective paddle.

Surface dive

K

Kickboard Another name for a float. It is usually held in the hands when practicing leg actions.

L

Lane marker A rope or wire, often with plastic discs on it, that runs the length of the pool and is used to stop people from swimming into each other's path.

Leg One complete section of a relay race. For example, in a 4 x 100 m relay, the four team members will each swim 100 m, or one leg, of the race.

Leisure pool A swimming pool specially designed for leisure activities.

Log roll A movement when a swimmer rotates, while horizontal in the water, with fully extended body, arms above the head, legs together.

M

Medley, Individual An event where competitors perform the following strokes over a set distance: butterfly, backstroke, breaststroke, and freestyle. The freestyle stroke cannot be one of the other three strokes.

Medley, Relay An event where teams compete against each other. Each team member swims a different stroke in the following order: backstroke, breaststroke, butterfly, and freestyle. The freestyle stroke cannot be one of the strokes already swum.

Mushroom float A float position when the swimmer is face down, with the body in a tucked position, and legs hugged to the body.

O

Oyster A figure of synchronized swimming when the swimmer submerges from a flat position on the surface by dropping the body down, with legs and hands towards the surface. The hands hold on to the ankles.

P

Pike A position adopted during the flight of some dives, when the swimmer's body momentarily bends at the hips.

Prone A swimming position where the swimmer lies on his or her front.

Propulsion Movement through the water as a result of leg or arm action.

Pull buoy A type of float that fits around a part of the body, enabling a swimmer to concentrate on another part. For example, pull buoys that fit on your legs help you to work on your arm techniques.

Push and glide position A position where the swimmer's body is fully extended so it is as streamlined as possible. It is used when pushing off from the poolside and gliding through the water.

R

Recovery The stage in a stroke sequence when the swimmer's legs or arms have finished the propulsive stage and are returning to their starting positions.

S

"S" pull An efficient backstroke arm action. The arm makes the shape of an "S" in the water. Also known as the bent arm action.

Screw kick An uneven leg kick used in breaststroke.

Sculling Propelling yourself through the water by moving your hands in small figure-of-eight movements.

Simultaneous strokes A term used to describe breaststroke and butterfly.

Star float A floating position where the swimmer stretches out on the surface of the water in the shape of a star.

Starting block A block on which swimmers stand to start a race. The block is attached to the poolside and has a nonslip surface.

Supine A swimming position where the swimmer lies on his or her back.

Surface dive A dive from the surface of the water, so that the swimmer is submerged.

T

Touch turn A racing turn used when swimming breaststroke and butterfly.

Track start A method of starting a race. The competitor gets into a position with one foot forward and one foot back and grips the starting block with his or her hands and toes. This start gives a big push-off.

Transition The period of time that you are under the water during a start or turn.

Treading water A way of staying afloat in the water. The legs usually perform vertical breaststroke and the arms scull close to the surface.

Floats

Goggles

Trickle breathing A breathing technique where air is released gradually before a new breath is taken.

Tub A shape in synchronized swimming when the swimmer performs turning movements by using the hands while holding a position with his or her head; shins and feet on the surface and the hips are dropped down.

Tumble turn A racing turn used in the crawl.

W

Wind-up start A start used in relay takeovers, where you build up momentum by circling your arms.

Star float

Index

A
action 21, 42

B
back paddle 21
backstroke 24-5, 32
backstroke start 31, 42
backward somersault 19
ballet leg 35, 42
Biondi, Matt 29
body roll 24, 42
Botsford, Beth 37
breaststroke 26-27, 30-31, 33
breathing 21, 22, 24, 28, 29
butterfly 28-29, 31, 33
  history of 11, 28

C
canoe scull 34
cartwheel 35
catch point 25, 26, 42
competition pool 14, 42
competitions 36-37
crawl 22-23, 30-31, 32-33

D
dive ring, weighted 13, 42
diving 14, 20-21, 30, 38
diving area 15, 42
dolphin chain 35, 42
dolphin kick 18, 28, 31, 42
drag 12, 42

E
Egerszegy, Krisztina 26-27
emergency float 41
entry point 31, 42
explosive breathing 22, 42

F
false start rope 14, 42
figures 34, 42
finals 36, 42
flat scull 34
floating 16
formations 35
forward somersault 18
freestyle relay 36, 42
front paddle 21, 42

G
glide position 17, 42
goggles 12, 13, 20
grab start 30, 42

H
hand mitt 13, 42
hand paddle 13, 42
heats 36, 42
high-lift style 27, 42
horizontal float 16, 42

I
International Swimming Cup, 1990 26, 28
intoeing 24, 43

K
kickboard 12, 13, 43
kneeling dive 30

L
lane marker 14, 43
leg 36, 43
legsuit 11
leisure pool 15, 43
Lewis, Hayley 28
log roll 20, 43

M
medleys 36, 43
mushroom float 16, 43

N
nutrition 15

O
Olympics 11, 31, 36, 37, 38, 39
open-water swimming 14
outdoor pool 14-15
oyster 34, 43

P
Paralympics 37
Perkins, Kieren 37
pike 30-31, 43
propulsion 21, 26, 43
pull buoy 12, 13, 43
push and glide 16-17, 26, 43
push off 32, 40

R
racing start 30-31
racing turn 32-33
recovery 25, 29, 43
rescues 41
reverse scull 34
Rolph, Susan 25
Rouse, Jeff 10, 24

S
"S" pull 24, 43
safety 14-15, 31, 40-41
screw kick 43

sculling 18-19, 34-35, 43
side bent knee link 35
simultaneous strokes 43
Smith, Michelle 22
snorkeling 38
somersaults 18-19
Spitz, Mark 11
standard scull 34
standing up 17
star float 16, 43
starting block 14, 15, 43
stationary sculling 18-19
surface dive 20-21, 43
surfing 38
sweat suits 13
swimming clubs 37
swimsuits 11, 12-13
swimming pools 14-15
synchronized swimming 34-35

T
torpedo scull 34
touch turn 32, 43
track start 30, 43
transition 30-31, 43
treading water 19, 43
triathlon 36
trickle breathing 22, 43
tub 34, 43
tumble turn 32, 43

U
underwater games 20

W
warming up 15, 23, 25, 27, 29
warning signs 15, 40
water confidence 20-21
water polo 38, 39
water safety 14-15, 31, 40-41
waterskiing 38, 39
Weissmuller, Johnny 11
whip kick 25
wind-up start 30, 43
windsurfing 38, 39

Useful addresses

Here are the addresses of some swimming organizations, which you may find useful.

United States Swimming &United States Olympic Committee on Swimming
One Olympic Plaza
Colorado Springs, CO 80909-5770
ph: 719/578-4578

US Diving
Pan American Plaza
201 S.Capitol Avenue, Suite 430
Indianpolis, IN 46225
ph: 317/237-5252

Synchronized Swimming
US Synchronized Swimming
Pan American Plaza
201 S.Capitol Avenue, Suite 510
Indianpolis, IN 46225

Amateur Athletic Association of the US, Inc.
3206 Prospect, Apt.#45
Cleveland, OH 44115
Attention: Todd Proa
ph: 216/391-6323

American Swimming Coaches Association
2101 North Andrews Avenue
Suite 107
Fort Lauderdale, FL 33311
ph: 954/563 4930

American Red Cross
150 Amsterdam Avenue
New York, NY 10023
ph: 212/787-1000

Marvin　Harry　Lisa　Greta　Melanie　Laura　Kaya　Jun　Annabelle

Acknowledgments

DK would like to thank the following people for their help in the production of this book:

With special thanks to: all the young swimmers for their skill, enthusiasm, and hard work; the swimmers' families; Alison Bell for advice on synchronized swimming; Putney Leisure Centre; Brigid Land and Andrew Jackson for assistance on the photo sessions; Hilary Gough (Swimming Development Officer at Wandsworth); Alan Guy and all the staff and children at Leander Swimming Club; Clare Brooker for lifeguard duties; Jenny Forest for the use of her pool; The Royal Life Saving Society UK for the use of their photos and valuable advice; the RYA–Windsurfing; British Water-ski; British Surfing Association; Noltan St Louis; Lesley Betts, Susan St Louis, Sophia Tampakopoulos, Claire Tindell for design

assistance; Patricia Grogan, Sarah Johnston, Stella Love for editorial assistance; Giles Powell-Smith for the jacket design.

Picture credits
key: b=bottom; l=left; r=right; c=center; t=top; a=above; b=below
Action Plus/Neale Haynes: 15br; /Mike Hewitt: 28cr; /Glyn Kirk: 36cr; /DPPI: 36b; /Peter Tarry: 39cl; All Action/Al Bello: 37tr; Allsport/Al Bello: 10tl, 10tr; /Shaun Botterill: 28bl, 39tl; /Simon Bruty: 14-15, 25tr, 27tr, 29br, 31cr; /Michael Cooper: 14bl; /Mike Hewitt: 22cl; /David Leach: 14t; /Graham Bool: 37cl; /Bob Martin: 36cl; /Markus Boesch: 38br; Christel Clear Marine

Photography/ Christel Clear: 40tr; Colorific: Robert Garvey: 40bl; Colorsport: 11bl, 38tr; /Andrew Cowie: 15bl, 37bl; Mary Evans Picture Library: 11cra; Werner Forman Archive/The British Museum, London: 11t; Dan Helms: 10cl, 10bc, 24cla; The Image Bank/Gianalberto Cigolini: 35clb; Popperfoto: 11cla; The Royal Life Saving Society: 41tl, 41bl; US Swimming/Charlie Snyder: 10cr; Speedo: 11br; Sporting Pictures (UK) Ltd: 32tr, 36tr; /John Carter: 39br; Telegraph Colour Library: 26bl, 40br, 38cl; Topham: 11bc; Alan Towse Photography: 37tl; John Walmsley: 12bl. Back jacket: Tony Duffy. Endpapers: Action Plus/Mike Hewitt.